Keystone
Species
in Nature

Keystone Species
that Live
in Forests

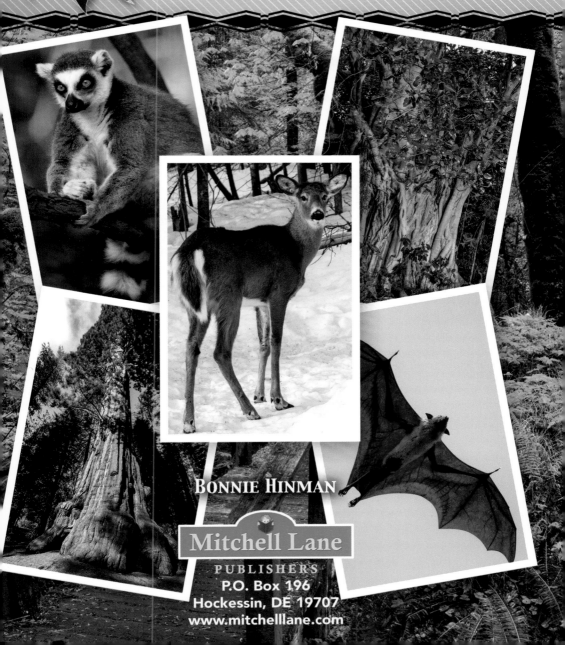

BONNIE HINMAN

Mitchell Lane
PUBLISHERS
P.O. Box 196
Hockessin, DE 19707
www.mitchelllane.com

PUBLISHERS

Printing   1   2   3   4   5   6   7   8

Keystone Species that Live in Deserts
Keystone Species that Live in Forests
Keystone Species that Live in Grasslands
Keystone Species that Live in the Mountains
Keystone Species that Live in Ponds, Streams, and Wetlands
Keystone Species that Live in the Sea and Along the Coastline

Library of Congress Cataloging-in-Publication Data
Hinman, Bonnie.
Keystone species that live in forests / by Bonnie Hinman.
    pages cm. — (A kid's guide to keystone species in nature)
Includes bibliographical references and index.
Audience: Ages 8 to 11.
Audience: Grades 3 to 6.
ISBN 978-1-68020-066-9 (library bound)
1. Keystone species—Juvenile literature. 2. Forest ecology—Juvenile literature. I. Title.
QH541.15.K48H5567 2015
577.2'6—dc23
                                        2015019270
eBook ISBN: 978-1-68020-067-6

PBP

Contents

Words in **bold** throughout can be found in the Glossary.

Introduction

Most arches built today contain a single building block at the top that is the most important piece. This special piece can be found in the arches of soaring cathedrals, doorways in temples, and even simple buildings made out of wooden blocks. It is called a keystone, and it holds everything else together. Remove the keystone and the building or doorway is likely to collapse.

The same thing is true in nature. Certain species of animals and plants are so important to their **ecosystems**, that if they disappear, the whole system may collapse. They are called keystone species.

Some keystone species are large, like coast redwood trees, while others are small, like ring-tailed lemurs (LEE-merz). But size doesn't matter in an ecosystem. All living

A keystone of a palace archway

White-tailed deer

things rely on other species to survive. A keystone species plays an especially large role that affects many different species in an ecosystem. Some keystone species are at the top of a huge ecosystem like the Greater Yellowstone Ecosystem, while others may affect a tiny ecosystem in a river or forest. Whether the ecosystem is big or small, the result of a keystone species disappearing or being greatly reduced is the same. Just like one falling domino can cause many others to fall, the loss of a keystone species can lead to the extinction of many other species.

Today scientists are focusing more attention on preserving the natural balance in ecosystems. Identifying and protecting keystone species is an important part of their work.

Chapter 1
RING-TAILED LEMUR

Lemurs (LEE-merz) look and act a lot like monkeys, but they are not monkeys. Lemurs and monkeys are both primates, however. This means they both have flexible thumbs, which allow them to grasp objects. Primates have eyes that face forward instead of facing the sides of their heads, and they have bigger brains than other mammals that are about the same size. Gorillas and chimpanzees are also primates, and so are humans.

Lemurs are **native** to Madagascar, a large island in the Indian Ocean, to the east of the coast of Mozambique in Africa. Madagascar is the fourth-largest island in the world. It is almost as big as Texas. Madagascar has many different ecosystems including rainforests, grasslands, and wetlands. According to the World Wildlife Fund, approximately "92 percent of [Madagascar's] mammals exist nowhere else on Earth."[1]

Lemurs are one of those mammals that only live on Madagascar. There are more than one hundred different species of lemurs living on the big island.[2] Ring-tailed lemurs live on the southern end of Madagascar. They like to live in dense forests near rivers and other sources of water. However, they can live in many different **habitats**,

Male ring-tailed lemurs use their long tails during "stink fights." They rub their tails across their wrists and chests, covering the tails with a smelly substance. They wave their tails in the air, using the scent to warn their opponent to back off. A good stink fight can last up to an hour.

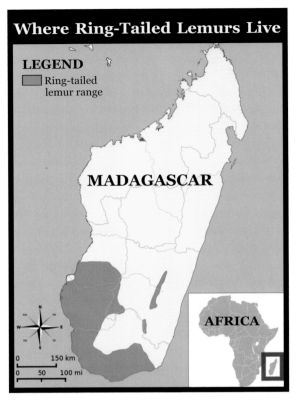

Where Ring-Tailed Lemurs Live

LEGEND
Ring-tailed lemur range

MADAGASCAR

AFRICA

0   150 km
0   50   100 mi

including dry areas far from forests. These animals are also able to **adapt** easily to a variety of foods and temperatures.

Ring-tailed lemurs get their name from their black-and-white-ringed tails. These tails can be from twenty-two inches to twenty-five inches (fifty-six to sixty-two centimeters) long— longer than their bodies! Their bodies are only fifteen to eighteen inches (thirty-nine to forty-six centimeters) long. They weigh about five pounds (2.2 kilograms) in the wild,[3] and sometimes more in captivity.

A ring-tailed lemur has a white face with black patches around its eyes and a black **snout**. It looks a little like a raccoon. Its back and legs are grayish-brown or reddish-brown and its stomach and feet are white. The ring-tailed lemur has large, bright yellow or amber eyes.

Ring-tailed lemurs spend more time on the ground than any other kind of lemur. Most lemurs live almost entirely in the treetops. Ring-tailed lemurs move through the trees, too, but they spend about one-third of their day on the ground running on all four legs. As they run, their long tails stand nearly straight up, curved only at the top.[4]

Ring-tailed lemurs live in troops, which are groups of three to thirty-five members. The leader of a ring-tailed lemur troop is a female. She and her relatives make up the permanent troop. Sometimes a troop includes females who are not related to the leader. Males often move from one troop to another once they are adults, while females usually stay in the troop where they were born.

A Lemur's Day

Ring-tailed lemurs have a daily routine that they follow. The troop sleeps together in one tree, or in several neighboring trees if they need more space. They spend the early morning hours moving around and taking sunbaths. A sunbathing ring-tailed lemur sits on the ground with its arms resting on its knees. The lemur leans back to let the sun warm its stomach and chest.

Breakfast often runs into lunch for the ring-tailed lemurs. They eat fruit, leaves, flowers, bark, and even insects. They particularly like tamarind (TAM-uh-rind) tree pods. These pods are important because they are available at times of the year when other food is not. Ring-tailed lemurs get water from the plants they eat, and they drink water from dew or rain on trees. They only drink water from the ground if no dew or rainwater is available in the trees.[5]

In the afternoons, the lemurs rest and groom each other. They use their tongues and teeth along with claws on their second toes to carefully comb through fur. A ring-tailed lemur often pairs up with another troop member for grooming. But they sometimes groom themselves.

When rest time is over, the ring-tailed lemurs go back to eating until it is time to move to their sleeping spot.

The females usually pick a couple of trees for sleeping. The troop spends the night in these trees. They do not sleep the whole time. They move around, do some more grooming, and maybe argue a bit.[6]

Ring-tailed lemurs mate in April or May and have their babies in August or September. Usually a female has one or two babies each year. Baby ring-tailed lemurs cling to their mothers' stomachs at first, and then ride on their mothers' backs once they are about one month old. They eat solid food by the time they are two months old, but keep nursing until they are four to six months old. Fathers do not help much with the babies when they are newborns, but other females help the new mother right away. Later both males and females in the troop look after the babies. Ring-tailed lemurs are fully grown at about eighteen months old, and can breed at two to

This female ring-tailed lemur may be carrying her own baby or it could be another troop member's baby. All the females in a troop help care for babies. This gives lemur mothers a chance to rest or look for food.

three years old. In the wild, they can live for eighteen to twenty years.[7]

A Key Role in Madagascar

Ring-tailed lemurs depend on tamarind trees for food when other sources are not available. But the tamarind trees also depend on the ring-tailed lemurs for reproduction. A seed that falls to the ground from a tamarind tree usually lands in a shady area under the tree's branches. Without enough sunlight, the seed can't germinate. However, when the ring-tailed lemurs eat tamarind pods, the seeds pass through the lemurs' bodies unharmed. When they land on the ground inside a pile of poop, the seeds often end up in a sunny area where they have a better chance of germinating.[8]

Fossas are the biggest predators of ring-tailed lemurs. They are **carnivorous** mammals that look a lot like a cross between a big cat and a weasel. They only live in Madagascar. Lemurs are the fossas' favorite food, making up over half of their diet. But the fossas also eat other animals, like snakes and mice. If lemurs were to disappear, the fossas would need to eat a lot more of these other animals to survive. The populations of those prey species might shrink, or they may even become extinct. With less food available, the fossas themselves might decline in number or die out.

The biggest threat to ring-tailed lemurs is humans. Ring-tailed lemurs are endangered and their population is decreasing. Part of the problem is that the forests they live in are being destroyed. Farmers in Madagascar cut and burn trees to clear land to grow their crops on. Others cut the trees for timber or charcoal to sell.

A fossa is a member of the mongoose family. Thanks to claws and flexible ankles, it can climb trees with ease. This makes it easy for a fossa to hunt a lemur, its favorite meal.

Hunting lemurs is illegal in Madagascar, but it has become more common recently. In 2009, Madagascar's president was forced out of office. For several years, the new government couldn't enforce **conservation** laws. Poor residents often killed the lemurs for food, or to sell their meat. Illegal logging also increased during this time.

A new president was elected in Madagascar in 2013; however, illegal logging and hunting continue. Conservation groups have different plans to save the island's wildlife. One plan is to encourage travelers to visit Madagascar to see the ring-tailed lemurs and other unique animals that live there. With more visitors on the island, the people of Madagascar will be able to earn money working in hotels and restaurants. Then they will not need to hunt lemurs or cut down trees for food or money.[9] Conservationists don't know yet whether this plan or other plans will work. The ring-tailed lemur's survival will depend on choices the people of Madagascar make in the future.

Madagascar's Stone Forest

The Tsingy de Bemaraha (ZING-ee day behm-ah-RA-ha) National Park and Reserve on the west side of Madagascar is home to a strange and beautiful stone formation. Scientists think that the **porous** limestone here was shaped by water. Underground water soaked the limestone and slowly dissolved its weakest areas until caves and tunnels formed. Eventually the roofs of these caves and tunnels collapsed. Left behind were narrow canyons with walls that formed pointed peaks. Over the years the limestone peaks continued to erode until they were razor-sharp. It became a "forest" of stone peaks. In Madagascar's language, Malagasy (mal-uh-GAS-ee), *tsingy* means, "Where one cannot walk barefoot."[10] Even with protective clothing and equipment, the sharp rocks can easily injure explorers. Still, many species live in the park. Humans who are brave enough to enter the tsingy often discover new species there.

Chapter 2

COAST REDWOOD

If you were to put the Statue of Liberty in a coast redwood forest and climb into her torch, you would still have to look up to see the tops of many coast redwood trees. The Statue of Liberty is 305 feet (93 meters) tall, while a coast redwood tree named Hyperion is over 379 feet (115 meters) tall. Hyperion is the tallest known living tree in the world.

Hyperion lives in a remote area of Redwood National Park in Northern California, about 325 miles (523 kilometers) north of San Francisco. Many other coast redwood trees that are nearly as tall as Hyperion live near California's Pacific coast.

There are three species of redwood trees in the world. Coast redwoods live along the central and northern coast of California and in the southwestern corner of Oregon. Giant sequoias are the second species. They live in the western Sierra Nevada mountain range in California. They have thicker trunks than coast redwoods, but they are not as tall. The third species, the dawn redwood, is native to central China. Dawn redwoods are much shorter than the other two redwood species.

Giant coast redwoods line a road in Jedediah Smith State Park near Crescent City, California. Next to the vehicles on this road, it's easy to see just how tall these coast redwoods are.

Coast redwood trees may be huge, but their cones are not. Each cone is about an inch long and contains a few dozen tiny seeds.

Redwoods are conifers (KOH-nuh-ferz). This means that they produce cones which contain their seeds. Other conifers include pines, spruces, and firs. Like most conifers, coast redwoods have needles for leaves. Coast redwoods shed some of their old needles in late summer, but are evergreen. Deep reddish bark and **heartwood** give all the redwoods their name.

Coast redwoods need a lot of water to survive and grow. They also grow best in a mild climate. The coasts of northern California and southern Oregon meet both of these needs. The average annual temperatures there range from 50 to 60 degrees Fahrenheit (10 to 16 degrees Celsius). The coast redwoods' homes receive from 25 to 122 inches (64 to 310 centimeters) of rain each year, mostly during the winter. When the rain disappears in summer, fog replaces it. Scientists say that fog is even more important than rain to the coast redwoods.[1]

Fog forms when warm summer air meets the cool Pacific waters. When the fog moves onto land, coast redwood trees use the fog's moisture. The trees' needles absorb some of the water directly from the fog. Moisture also **condenses** on the needles and drips to the soil below. Many other plants are able to use this water once it's in the soil.[2]

Growing and Surviving

Coast redwood trees may grow as much as three feet (one meter) per year if they have the right amount of water and sunlight. In less than perfect conditions, they grow more slowly.[3] Since they live a long time, coast redwoods have plenty of time to grow. Scientists estimate that the trees may live more than two thousand years, although most redwoods alive today are much younger.[4]

Even the tallest trees in the world can't keep growing forever. It is more difficult for a coast redwood to send water and

During the summer, fog is a common sight in a coast redwood forest. The fog doesn't just provide moisture to the trees directly, it also blocks some of the summer sun. Without fog, the strong sunlight would cause much-needed water to evaporate from the forests.

nutrients to the branches and needles at the very top of the tree. Scientists say that coast redwoods probably can't grow taller than about 427 feet (130 meters).[5]

Coast redwoods are also resistant to insects, **fungi**, and fire. Their wood is high in tannin, a substance that is poisonous to insects and prevents the growth of fungi. Older coast redwoods have bark as thick as twelve inches (thirty centimeters).[6] This thick bark combined with the tannin allows them to survive fires. A fire seldom kills a mature coast redwood, although it may create hollows in the tree.

Coast redwoods reproduce in several ways. One way is by growing inch-long cones that contain tiny seeds. Each tree produces as many as one hundred thousand seeds a year, but very few of those seeds germinate.[7] Sometimes a tree reproduces when a branch breaks off of the parent tree and falls to the ground. This branch can grow roots and become a new tree.

Reproduction by sprouting is more successful for the coast redwood. Sprouts can grow from the stump or roots of a tree, whether it is healthy, damaged, or cut down. These sprouts connect to the existing roots and sometimes form a ring around the parent tree or stump. Sprouts grow a lot faster than seedlings. A sprout may grow as much as six feet (1.8 meters) in its first year.[8]

A Hidden Community

Scientists have discovered that a whole community of plants and animals lives in the **canopies** of mature coast redwood trees. The needles that fall from the upper branches settle on large branches below. This foliage collects and **decomposes** until it forms soil. Seeds root in this soil and germinate there. Trees such as tanbark oak and western hemlock grow in the canopies of the coast redwoods. Huckleberry and gooseberry bushes grow there, too. These trees and bushes that grow at the tops of redwoods provide food and homes to beetles, crickets, earthworms, salamanders, and millipedes. Birds like the

The Save the Redwoods League was organized in 1918 to protect and restore redwood forests. Recent scientific research funded by the group showed that giant sequoias and coast redwoods in the northern parts of their ranges have been growing more quickly since the 1970s than ever before. Researchers believe that this could be because the temperatures there have been increasing, so the trees have a longer growing season.[9]

bald eagle and peregrine falcon make their nests in the canopy communities.[10]

Many mature coast redwood trees have survived fires during their long lifetimes. The hollows that are left from these fires become hidden nesting places for birds. Vaux's swifts, violet-green swallows, and pygmy nuthatches all make their homes and lay their eggs here, out of sight from predators.[11] Without the oldest, tallest coast redwood trees, these plants and animals that depend on them might disappear.

When American settlers moved to California in the 1800s, they quickly discovered that coast redwood timber could resist damage from insects, fungi, and fire. This made the wood very valuable to them, and they began cutting the trees to use for construction. It is estimated that 5 percent of the original coast redwood forest remains today.[12] Young trees have regrown, but only the oldest trees can support large communities of animals and plants.

Coast redwoods are endangered and their numbers are decreasing.[13] Although most of the land that is home to the original forests is now protected from logging, the future of the coast redwoods is still uncertain. The changing climate may soon become a problem for the trees. Today there is 33 percent less fog in the redwood forests than there was one hundred years ago.[14] If the loss of fog continues, the redwoods may not be able to survive.

Conservation groups and governments are now working to buy and protect more coast redwood land. They hope to save this important species and all the plants and animals that depend on it.

Recreational Tree Climbing

Tree climbing is a sport growing in popularity among people of all ages. Technical tree climbers use ropes and harnesses to climb trees. They also use safety gear to protect themselves and the trees they climb. Formed in 1983, Tree Climbers International is an organization that promotes safe tree climbing. They offer classes and information about tree climbing. TCI climbers learn that they must always wear helmets and stay attached to the rope system while in a tree. They never use spikes to climb since this would damage the tree. Almost anyone can become a tree climber after learning some basic techniques.

Chapter 3
WHITE-TAILED DEER

When you walk through a wooded area in the spring, you might notice a tiny movement in a pile of brush nearby. You look closely at the pile, but see nothing except tree branches and bushes. However, if you look more carefully, you might finally see that there is a tiny animal stretched out on the ground under the brush. You have discovered the hiding place for a white-tailed deer baby or fawn.

White-tailed deer mothers hide their newborn fawns in thick cover while the mothers go away to feed for a few hours. The fawns' fur is brown with white spots, which allows them to blend into the forest floor. A fawn may not even move if you get close to it. But you should never try to touch or move a fawn. Its mother won't return if she senses danger.

There are few baby animals cuter than a white-tailed deer fawn. Their parents are beautiful animals as well, with their slender legs, strong bodies, and curved necks. However, these **stately** animals are causing a lot of trouble in forests and woodlands.

A keystone species is one that affects a large number of other species in an ecosystem. Most keystone species

A white-tailed deer fawn's spots fade gradually until they are completely gone by the beginning of a fawn's first winter. The spots serve as camouflage for the newborn fawn as it stretches out on the forest floor to hide from predators.

improve or maintain the natural balance of plants and animals in their habitats. But when there are too many of them, the white-tailed deer does just the opposite. The deer can destroy the natural balance in its habitat.

White-Tailed Deer Basics

White-tailed deer live in North America and South America, from Canada in the north to Bolivia in the south. On these two continents, there are thirty-eight subspecies living in different regions.[1] White-tailed deer are found in many different habitats including forests, farmlands, and swamps. If they could choose anywhere to live, it would likely be a forest or area with thick bushes that is also near open land. They use trees and underbrush to hide, and eat where the forest and the open land meet.

White-tailed deer eat many different kinds of plants. They eat **forbs**, berries, acorns, hickory nuts, grass, and twigs and leaves from trees and bushes. One study in Arizona showed that white-tailed deer eat more than 610 different plant species in that state.[2]

The fur of a white-tailed deer changes color depending on the season. Different subspecies also have slightly different colors. Usually they are reddish brown in the summer and grayish brown in the winter. Their fur is white around their nose, eyes, ears, chin, and throat, and on their bellies and the insides of their legs. The white fur under their tails gives them their name.

Some subspecies of white-tailed deer are much larger than others. The largest deer are usually found in the cold, northern regions. They can weigh 300 pounds (140 kilograms) or more. The smallest subspecies are found in warm climates. They sometimes weigh less than 70 pounds (30 kilograms). An adult white-tailed deer will be larger than average if lots of good food is available where it lives. Females, or does, are smaller than males, which are called bucks.

Where White-Tailed Deer Live

North America

South America

LEGEND
White-tailed deer range

White-tailed deer live within **home ranges**. A typical home range might be about one square mile (2.6 square kilometers). But a deer's home range can be much larger if good food is hard to find. Females tend to have smaller ranges than males do.[3]

Fawns

In northern areas, white-tailed deer mate in the fall or winter and the fawns are born about six to seven months later. Near the equator, mating occurs year-round. Young females usually have one baby at a time, while older does often have two or even three babies. Fawns are able to stand and walk right after birth. For the first few weeks, the fawns remain in hiding while their mothers return to nurse them several times a day. At about a month old, a fawn begins to follow its mother as she looks for food. Fawns nibble at plants, but continue to nurse from their mothers until they are eight to ten weeks old.[4]

Female fawns may stay with their mothers for about two years, but males generally leave after a year or so.

These young fawns' long legs make it hard to reach the ground to eat the tender plants there, but later their long legs will make it easier to eat tree branches or tall bushes.

Most white-tailed deer first mate when they are about a year and a half old, but timing can vary.[5] Some does may mate at about seven months old.

Predators of white-tailed deer include mountain lions, coyotes, bears, gray wolves, jaguars, and humans. The deer have good eyesight and hearing but depend on smell to let them know when it is time to run. They can leap and run through thick plants to escape danger.[6] Deer hunting is a popular sport, and people also hunt deer for meat.

Deer Everywhere

With so many people hunting white-tailed deer, one would think that there would be a shortage of them. However, the opposite is true. There are too many deer throughout North America.

When Europeans first arrived in North America, there were far fewer white-tailed deer than there are today. Hunters killed many coyotes and gray wolves, leaving the deer with fewer natural predators. Settlers began clearing forest areas for wood and land, so there were many more areas where forest and open land met. This created new homes for white-tailed deer. Through the nineteenth century, the deer populations were kept under control because hunters killed them also. But in the twentieth century, the US government changed laws to protect the deer. The population of white-tailed deer exploded. There may be more than eleven million white-tailed deer in the United States today.[7]

White-tailed deer can eat a lot of plants. They eat young trees and other plants or branches up to about five or six feet (1.5 to 1.8 meters) off the ground. Studies have shown that when there are too many white-tailed deer in an area, many of the plants they like to eat disappear completely. Other plants then take over the forest.

Removing certain species of plants from an area also affects the other animals that live there. Without those specific plants and trees, many birds have no place to make nests. Other animals that eat the same plants and trees can't find enough food. They may die or leave the area. Small predators cannot find the prey they need so they leave, too.

Scientists in New York studied the effects of a large white-tailed deer population in that area. They found that wherever there were too many white-tailed deer, white-footed mice could not survive. Both species eat acorns, and the deer may have eaten most of the acorns before the mice could. The deer may have also eaten many of the plants that gave the mice places to hide from predators. White-footed mice eat gypsy moths and keep their population under control. When the mice disappeared from an area, large numbers of moths were able to live there.[8] Gypsy moths eat the leaves of trees and other plants. When these moths eat too many leaves from a single tree, the tree can die. The large population of white-tailed deer caused problems for many species

With the explosion of the white-tailed deer population, it is not unusual for deer to be found near parking lots or homes. Deer in populated areas are dangerous to the people who live there, and are also in danger themselves. When a vehicle hits a deer, it can kill the deer and the people inside the vehicle.

in their New York ecosystem, not just for the plants and trees they ate.

Hunting regulations have changed in the United States, and today more white-tailed deer can be hunted legally. This may help lower the number of deer in North America, but once an ecosystem is out of balance it can be difficult to bring the balance back. Conservationists will likely be working to solve the problems caused by white-tailed deer for many years to come.

How to Talk to a White-Tailed Deer

You can talk to a white-tailed deer all day long and he or she won't reply—at least not with words. However, white-tailed deer do communicate—in addition to sounds and smells, they use their bodies. Deer use several different movements and body positions to let other deer know what they want to say. They will stomp their front feet to alert other deer to danger or to scare off a predator. The tail flag is a tail-waving motion that a deer uses as it runs away. This is also a danger warning. Flicking the tail from side to side says that the deer is getting ready to move. When a deer lays its ears back along its neck, it is warning other deer to stay away. If one deer touches its nose to another deer's nose, it is "poking" the deer to tell it which way to move. A buck sometimes lowers his head and points his antlers at another buck. This is called an antler threat. If the other buck does the same, the fight is on.[9]

This deer's laid-back ears say, "Stay away."

Chapter 4
STRANGLER FIG

This tree has a scary name, but don't worry—it will not be grabbing you if you walk through a tropical forest. The strangler fig's victims are other trees.

Strangler fig trees belong to the Ficus (FAHY-kuhs) **genus**. There are about one thousand different species of ficus.[1] They live all over the world in tropical and subtropical areas like rainforests. Strangler fig is the common name for a group of ficus species that use other trees to support them as they grow.

Strangler figs are tall canopy trees, but they don't start their lives the way most other trees do. Monkeys, birds, and other animals drop strangler fig seeds on branches near the tops of other trees. Seeds germinate where they landed. The new plants grow and form roots, which hang down into the air or along the trunk of the support tree.

At first the figs grow slowly in their airy treetop homes. At this stage they are epiphytes (EP-uh-fahyts), which we sometimes call air plants. Air plants grow on other plants and have no roots in the ground. Their food comes from the sun, air, and rainwater.

This strangler fig is no longer an epiphyte. Its roots have reached the ground, and it gets its nutrients from the soil. This has allowed it to put down a large number of roots, which are nearly completely surrounding the host tree.

Into the Ground

Strangler fig roots grow downward along the trunk of the support tree. Some roots grow straight down from their source in the canopy. Eventually all of these roots reach the forest floor and grow into the ground there.

Once the roots reach the forest floor, nutrients in the soil help the figs to grow much faster. The roots become thicker, and they twist around the support tree. Soon the strangler fig roots cover the support tree's trunk.

It looks like the strangler fig is choking the support tree to death, and in some ways this is true. The support tree's trunk cannot grow wider, since it is surrounded by the strangler fig. But what usually kills support trees is a lack of sunlight and nutrients. The leaves and branches at the top of the fig tree have grown quickly. The top of the fig tree crowds out the other canopy trees as they compete for sunlight. The fig tree's roots pull nutrients from the soil that the support tree would otherwise use. The support tree may die and rot. All that is left of it is the hollow column inside the strangler fig where it once lived.

Reproduction

Strangler fig trees do not have any visible flowers like most fruit trees do. Birds, insects, or winds usually pollinate fruit trees by moving pollen from flower to flower. Fig trees have flowers, but they are on the inside of the immature fruit. Without visible flowers, fig trees have a different plan for pollination. A tiny wasp does the job.

When the time is right for fig tree pollination, the tree sends out a special smell that attracts female wasps. Each species of fig attracts a certain species of wasp.[2] When a female wasp arrives at an immature fig fruit, she burrows inside through a tiny opening in the small ball. It is a tight fit and she usually loses her wings and antennae as she squeezes inside. The wasp has arrived with pollen either in small pockets or stuck to its body. Once inside the immature fruit she moves about, laying eggs and leaving pollen behind. She then dies inside the fruit.

The eggs hatch into male and female wasps. The males have no wings and only have two jobs to complete. They mate with the females inside the fruit. Once that is done, they chew a hole through the fig wall so the females can escape from the fruit. They die soon after, still inside the fruit. The females fly away with loads of pollen to find another fig tree and the cycle begins again. This cycle is an example of mutualism—a relationship between two species that benefits both species.

Once the female wasps fly away, the fruit that is left behind ripens. It then attracts monkeys, birds, and other animals, who eat the fruit and seeds. The birds fly over the forest or perch in tree branches, and monkeys swing through the treetops. The animals drop the undigested seeds in their poop on canopy tree branches. The seeds sprout there high above the ground.

Moving the fig seeds away from the mother tree is important because the forest floor is dark. The large canopies don't allow much light to reach the bottom of the forest. It is not easy for a new plant to sprout there. Therefore, the strangler figs also depend on the animals who eat their fruit to **disperse** their seeds.

Giving Life to the Forests

Over 1,200 species of animals all over the world eat figs.[3] These species include animals like pigeons, parrots, monkeys, and bats. Figs make up more than 90 percent of the diets of some bird species.[4] Unlike most fruit trees, strangler and other fig species produce fruit more than once a year. The different fig species, and even different fig trees of the same species, also bear fruit at different times. Because of this, figs are available year-round. At certain times of year, figs may be the only trees producing food for hundreds of animals. Many animals prefer figs to other fruits, and scientists have discovered that figs have more nutrients like calcium than most other fruits do.[5]

Aside from providing food, strangler figs also provide homes to many animals. The hollow columns that form where support trees had been are hidden shelters. As both food and shelter for many species, strangler figs are important keystone species in any forest where they live.

Strangler fig trees are still abundant almost everywhere. However, habitat destruction by fire, logging, human population growth, or climate change could threaten the strangler figs in the future. For a strangler fig to reproduce, there must be another fig tree of the same species close by. The female wasp must be able to find a second tree quickly to pollinate its flowers. If enough forest is destroyed, this might not happen, and the female wasps may die before they reach another fig tree. Then the figs would be unable to reproduce.

As a vital part of a huge food cycle for hundreds of species, strangler figs give life to many, even as they kill other trees. In the tropical and subtropical forests, their role is key to preserving the balance of nature. By keeping strangler figs in their homes, we can help ensure that this balance is maintained.

Cloud Forests

Cloud forests are forests that "catch" clouds. Clouds are tiny droplets of water in the air. When the clouds meet the treetops, the water condenses into droplets that fall into the forest below. It rains on cloud forests, too, but clouds provide as much as 60 percent of the water in a cloud forest.[6] Cloud forests can grow anywhere that clouds regularly meet the treetops, but most are found in tropical areas. There are cloud forests in Mexico, Central America, and tropical South America. Southeast Asia and Africa also have many cloud forests.[7] Since clouds are usually high in the sky, cloud forests are often on high ground. Ferns, orchids, and mosses grow quickly in a cloud forest. There is also lots of ground water in cloud forests, which people send through pipes to nearby farms and cities.

A cloud forest near Mindo, Ecuador

Chapter 5

FLYING FOX

What does a flying fox look like? You might be confused because the last time you saw a picture of a fox, it probably did not have wings. A flying fox is a kind of bat. Bats have small faces with large eyes and pointed ears, so they look a little like foxes. A flying fox is a mammal like a regular fox, but that is about the only thing they have in common.

There are more than one thousand bat species on Earth. The only mammal family with more members is the **rodent** family. All bats play important roles in keeping our ecosystems healthy. However, bats do not have a good reputation among humans. Many people think they are dangerous.

There are two kinds of bats: microbats and megabats. Most of the bat species on Earth are microbats, which are usually smaller than megabats. Megabats use smell and eyesight to find their favorite foods of pollen, nectar, and fruit. Microbats use **echolocation** to find the insects that they like to eat. Megabats live in the tropical and subtropical regions of Europe, Africa, Asia, and Australia, while microbats live everywhere except the Arctic and Antarctic.

This black flying fox lives near Brisbane in Queensland, Australia. The black flying fox is the largest flying fox species in Australia. Its wingspan can be as large as 6 feet (1.8 meters). These big bats primarily live in tropical, mangrove, and swamp forests, but can also live in urban areas.

Flying foxes are megabats, and they are sometimes called fruit bats. There are more than 180 species of flying foxes.[1] Bats are the only mammals that have true wings and can fly. Their wings are covered with skin and supported by four fingers.

Flying foxes have large chests with strong muscles to power their wings during flight. Their eyes are big, which may help explain why they have such good vision. Flying foxes like to hang upside down to sleep. They have special hip sockets that allow them to do this.[2] They also have claws on their feet that are able to lock onto a branch. The feet will stay locked until the flying fox straightens its body to fly. Flying foxes can continue to hang from a branch even after they die.[3]

Indian flying fox

Flying Fox Camps

Flying foxes **roost** together in camps during the daytime. There can be thousands of these bats in a single camp. Flying foxes are nocturnal. When the sun begins to appear at dawn, the animals return from feeding to roost together. Sometimes the bats live in a permanent camp all year. Other camps may be temporary. Flying foxes will stay in a camp only as long as there is a good supply of food nearby.

Flying foxes are sociable and use their daytime camps for more than sleep. They groom themselves and each other, take care of babies, and argue. Each species has its own calls that it uses for communication. Grey-headed flying foxes use more than thirty sounds to communicate with each other.[4] Each bat returns to a certain space on a branch daily. Older or higher-ranking bats roost higher in the tree branches.[5]

Most flying foxes only have one baby per year. Babies are called pups. The mother hangs right side up for the birth and catches the pup as it is born. Baby flying foxes are born with their eyes open. A pup attaches itself to Mom by clamping its claws to her fur and its mouth to her nipple. The mother flies out to feed at night with the baby clinging to her belly. When the pup gets too heavy for her to carry, she leaves it at camp while she searches for food.

As the pups get older, they begin learning to fly. Soon they start to fly with the adults to find food. The pups continue to nurse until they are up to four months old, although the exact timing is different for each species. The mother may take care of them for a little longer after they are weaned.

Flying foxes are ready to breed when they are about a year and a half to three years old. Females mature earlier than males do. Some species of flying foxes may live as long as thirty years. However, most flying foxes don't live to be more than ten to fifteen years old in the wild.

Helping the Plants

In the forests where they live, flying foxes perform two important jobs for many plants. One of those jobs is dispersing seeds. When they eat fruits, they may spit out the seeds or eat them. When they are eaten, the seeds pass through the flying foxes' digestive systems and come out in droppings. Either way, seeds often land far away from their parent trees, since the bats may travel many miles looking for food. If the seeds simply fell to the ground underneath the parent tree, they might not get enough sunlight to be able to germinate.

Flying foxes eat lots of nectar and pollen. Some pollen also sticks to the bats' fur, then gets carried to the next tree where they eat. There, the blossoms are pollinated so seeds can be produced. Flying foxes can carry pollen further than many other pollinating species. If two trees of the same species are farther apart than a bee or wasp would travel, the trees will depend on flying foxes for pollination.

There are many threats to flying foxes, but most of them are from humans. People often intentionally harm the animals by shooting them, sometimes to stop them from eating fruit. In some places, people hunt the bats for meat. People destroy camps to force the flying foxes to leave. Cutting down trees for wood and land leaves these bats with fewer places to live, as well.

Many species of flying foxes are listed as endangered or threatened. In some places, shooting flying foxes is illegal. Educating people about the importance of flying foxes can help keep the animals safe. People can also learn how to protect their fruit trees with nets that keep the bats out without harming them.[6] Conservationists are working to identify and protect forests that are home to flying fox populations. Still, in some areas governments are not acting to save these important keystone species. Without flying foxes, our forests and other habitats will gradually change and vanish. We cannot afford to let that happen.

Vampire Bats

Legends about bats tell of creatures that suck blood from human victims. It is a good story, but only partly true. Out of more than a thousand species of bats, only three drink blood. The common vampire bat, the hairy-legged vampire bat, and the white-winged vampire bat all live on blood alone. These microbat species live in North and South America. A vampire bat might drink human blood if it couldn't find anything else. However, these bats prefer other kinds of blood. Common vampire bats like cow, goat, and horse blood. Hairy-legged vampire bats like bird blood. White-winged vampire bats drink both mammal and bird blood. Vampire bats do not suck blood. They lick it up after using their sharp teeth to make a small cut on their victim's body. Vampire bats feed for about twenty to thirty minutes at a time. They can drink half of their body weight in blood during this time.

A common vampire bat

CHAPTER NOTES

Chapter 1: Ring-Tailed Lemur
    1. Tom Dillon and Rachel Kramer, "Madagascar," World Wildlife Fund, http://worldwildlife.org/places/Madagascar
    2. Madeleine Lewis, "Cuppa & Chat With . . . Dr. Russ Mittermeier, World's Biggest Lemur Fan!" Virgin Unite, October 31, 2014, http://www.virgin.com/unite/leadership-and-advocacy/cuppa-chat-with-dr-russ-mittermeier-worlds-biggest-lemur-fan
    3. San Diego Zoo Global, "Ring-Tailed Lemur (*Lemur catta*) Fact Sheet, 2009," updated February 25, 2015, http://ielc.libguides.com/sdzg/factsheets/ringtailedlemur
    4. Kristina Cawthon Lang, "Ring-Tailed Lemur: *Lemur catta*," National Primate Research Center, University of Wisconsin-Madison, September 21, 2005, modified November 21, 2011, http://pin.primate.wisc.edu/factsheets/entry/ring-tailed_lemur
    5. San Diego Zoo Global, "Ring-Tailed Lemur (*Lemur catta*) Fact Sheet, 2009."
    6. Ibid.
    7. Ibid.
    8. A.S. Mertl-Millhollen, et al., "Tamarind Tree Seed Dispersal by Ring-Tailed Lemurs," *Primates*, October 2011, pp. 391–396, http://www.ncbi.nlm.nih.gov/pubmed/21629992
    9. IUCN Red List of Threatened Species, "Emergency Three-Year Action Plan for Lemurs," February 21, 2014, http://www.iucnredlist.org/news/emergency-three-year-action-plan-for-lemurs
    10. Neil Shea, "Living on a Razor's Edge," *National Geographic*, November 2009, http://ngm.nationalgeographic.com/2009/11/stone-forest/shea-text

Chapter 2: Coast Redwood
    1. David F. Olson, Jr., Douglass F. Roy, and Gerald A. Walters, "Sequoia *sempervirens* (D. Don) Endl.: Redwood," in Russell M. Burns and Barbara H. Honkala, *Silvics of North America*, Volume 1 (Washington, DC: US Department of Agriculture, Forest Service, 1990), http://www.na.fs.fed.us/pubs/silvics_manual/Volume_1/sequoia/sempervirens.htm
    2. Dr. Paul D. Haemig, "Ecology of the Coast Redwood," Ecology.Info, 2012, http://www.ecology.info/redwood.htm
    3. California Department of Parks and Recreation, "About Coast Redwoods," http://www.parks.ca.gov/?page_id=22257
    4. Save the Redwoods League, "Coast Redwoods," http://www.savetheredwoods.org/redwoods/coast-redwoods/
    5. Save the Redwoods League, "What Limits Redwood Height?" http://www.savetheredwoods.org/grant/what-limits-redwood-height/
    6. Save the Redwoods League, "Coast Redwoods."
    7. California Department of Parks and Recreation, "About Coast Redwoods."
    8. Olson, Roy, and Walters, "*Sequoia sempervirens* (D. Don) Endl.: Redwood."
    9. Save the Redwoods League, "Past, Present and Future of Redwoods: A Redwood Ecology & Climate Symposium," 2013, p. 8, https://www.savetheredwoods.org/wp-content/uploads/RCCI-Symposium-2013-Abstracts.pdf
    10. Haemig, "Ecology of the Coast Redwood."
    11. Ibid.
    12. Save the Redwoods League, "Coast Redwoods."
    13. A. Farjon and R. Schmid, "*Sequoia sempervirens*," The IUCN Red List of Threatened Species, 2013, http://www.iucnredlist.org/details/34051/0
    14. Haemig, "Ecology of the Coast Redwood."

Chapter 3: White-Tailed Deer
    1. Robin J. Innes, "Species: *Odocoileus virginianus*," US Department of Agriculture, Forest Service, Rocky Mountain Research Station, Fire Sciences Laboratory, 2013, http://www.fs.fed.us/database/feis/animals/mammal/odvi/all.html
    2. Ibid.

CHAPTER NOTES

3. Maryland Department of Natural Resources, Wildlife and Heritage Service, "White-Tailed Deer Biology (*Odocoileus virginianus*)," http://dnr2.maryland.gov/wildlife/Pages/hunt_trap/wtdeerbiology.aspx

4. Tanya Dewey, "*Odocoileus virginianus*: White-Tailed Deer," University of Michigan Museum of Zoology, *Animal Diversity Web*, 2003, http://animaldiversity.org/accounts/Odocoileus_virginianus

5. Ibid.

6. Ibid.

7. S. Gallina and H. Lopez Arevalo, "*Odocoileus virginianus*," IUCN Red List of Threatened Species, 2008, http://www.iucnredlist.org/details/42394/0

8. T.P. Rooney, "Deer Impacts on Forest Ecosystems: A North American Perspective," *Forestry*, vol. 74, no. 3, 2001, p. 206, http://www.botany.wisc.edu/waller/PDFs/Rooney2001.pdf

9. T.R. Michels, "White-Tailed Deer Communication," Trinity Mountain Outdoors, http://www.trmichels.com/WhitetailCommunication.htm

Chapter 4: Strangler Fig

1. A.T.J. Ogunkunle and F.A. Oladele, "Leaf Epidermal Studies in Some Nigerian Species of *Ficus* L. (Moraceae)," *Plant Systematics and Evolution*, 2008, vol. 274, p. 209, https://www.unilorin.edu.ng/publications/oladele/LEAF%20EPIDERMAL%20STUDIES%20IN%20SOME%20NIGERIAN%20SPECIES%20OF%20FICUS%20L.%20.pdf

2. Beatriz Moisset, "Fig Wasps," United States Department of Agriculture, Forest Service, http://www.fs.fed.us/wildflowers/pollinators/pollinator-of-the-month/fig_wasp.shtml

3. Rhett D. Harrison, "Figs and the Diversity of Tropical Rainforests," *BioScience*, December 2005, vol. 55, no. 12, p. 1053.

4. Mike Shanahan, Samson So, Stephen G. Compton, and Richard Corlett, "Fig-Eating by Vertebrate Frugivores: A Global Review," *Biological Reviews*, 2001, vol. 76, p. 544.

5. Margaret Kinnaird, "In Indonesia, One Nutritious Fruit Is the Wild Fuel that Runs the Rain Forest," *National Wildlife*, January 1, 2000, http://www.nwf.org/News-and-Magazines/National-Wildlife/Animals/Archives/2000/Big-on-Figs.aspx

6. Community Cloud Forest Conservation, "Cloud Forest," http://www.cloudforestconservation.org/cloud_forest/

7. San Francisco Botanical Garden, "What Are Cloud Forests?" http://www.sfbotanicalgarden.org/cf/cf/

Chapter 5: Flying Fox

1. Francisca C. Almeida, et al., "Evolutionary Relationships of the Old World Fruit Bats (Chiroptera, Pteropodidae): Another Star Phylogeny?" *BMC Evolutionary Biology*, 2001, http://www.ncbi.nlm.nih.gov/pmc/articles/PMC3199269/pdf/1471-2148-11-281.pdf

2. Kenneth Cody Luzynski, Emily Margaret Sluzas, and Megan Marie Wallen, "Pteropodidae: Old World Fruit Bats," University of Michigan Museum of Zoology, *Animal Diversity Web*, April 19, 2009, http://animaldiversity.org/accounts/Pteropodidae/

3. Nicola Markus, "'Foxes' That Fly," *International Wildlife*, July/August 2001, vol. 31, issue 4, p. 22, Ebsco Host, Academic Search Elite.

4. State Government Victoria, Department of Environment and Primary Industries, "Flying-Foxes," http://www.depi.vic.gov.au/environment-and-wildlife/wildlife/flying-foxes

5. Markus, "'Foxes' That Fly."

6. Animals Australia, "Flying Foxes," http://www.animalsaustralia.org/issues/flying-foxes.php

WORKS CONSULTED

Almeida, Francisca C., Norberto P. Giannini, Rob DeSalle, and Nancy B. Simmons. "Evolutionary Relationships of the Old World Fruit Bats (*Chiroptera, Pteropodidae*): Another Star Phylogeny?" *BMC Evolutionary Biology*, 2001. http://www.ncbi.nlm.nih.gov/pmc/articles/PMC3199269/pdf/1471-2148-11-281.pdf

Anderson, Rebecca. "*Lemur catta*: Ring-Tailed Lemur." University of Michigan Museum of Zoology, *Animal Diversity Web*, June 7, 1999. http://animaldiversity.org/accounts/Lemur_catta/

Animals Australia. "Flying Foxes." http://www.animalsaustralia.org/issues/flying-foxes.php

Bat Conservation International. "Bats Are: Important." http://www.batcon.org/index.php/why-bats/bats-are/bats-are-important

Bradford, Alina. "Facts About Bats." *Live Science*, August 8, 2014. http://www.livescience.com/28272-bats.html

California Department of Parks and Recreation. "About Coast Redwoods." http://www.parks.ca.gov/?page_id=22257

Cawthon Lang, Kristina. "Ring-Tailed Lemur: *Lemur catta*." National Primate Research Center, University of Wisconsin-Madison, September 21, 2005, modified November 21, 2011. http://pin.primate.wisc.edu/factsheets/entry/ring-tailed_lemur

Community Cloud Forest Conservation. "Cloud Forest." http://www.cloudforestconservation.org/cloud_forest/

Dewey, Tanya. "*Odocoileus virginianus*: White-Tailed Deer." University of Michigan Museum of Zoology, *Animal Diversity Web*, 2003. http://animaldiversity.org/accounts/Odocoileus_virginianus

Dillon, Tom, and Rachel Kramer. "Madagascar." World Wildlife Fund. http://worldwildlife.org/places/Madagascar

Farjon, A., and R. Schmid. "*Sequoia sempervirens*." The IUCN Red List of Threatened Species, 2013. http://www.iucnredlist.org/details/34051/0

Gallina, S., and H. Lopez Arevalo. "*Odocoileus virginianus*." IUCN Red List of Threatened Species, 2008. http://www.iucnredlist.org/details/42394/0

Haemig, Dr. Paul D. "Ecology of the Coast Redwood." Ecology.Info, 2012. http://www.ecology.info/redwood-2.htm

Harrison, Rhett D. "Figs and the Diversity of Tropical Rainforests." *BioScience*, December 2005, vol. 55, no. 12, pp. 1053-1064.

Humboldt Redwoods State Park. "Redwoods." http://humboldtredwoods.org/redwoods

Innes, Robin J. "Species: *Odocoileus virginianus*." US Department of Agriculture, Forest Service, Rocky Mountain Research Station, Fire Sciences Laboratory, 2013. http://www.fs.fed.us/database/feis/animals/mammal/odvi/all.html

IUCN Red List of Threatened Species. "Emergency Three-Year Action Plan for Lemurs." February 21, 2014. http://www.iucnredlist.org/news/emergency-three-year-action-plan-for-lemurs

Jones, Eileen. "*Sequoia sempervirens*: Trial by Fire." *Wildcare*, August 2012. http://www.wildcarebayarea.org/site/PageServer?pagename=eNews_August2012_Redwoods&printer_friendly=1

Kennedy, Heather. "Ring-tailed Lemur: *Lemur catta*." Tree of Life Web Projects, 2008. http://tolweb.org/treehouses/?treehouse_id=4730

Kinnaird, Margaret. "In Indonesia, One Nutritious Fruit Is the Wild Fuel that Runs the Rain Forest." *National Wildlife*, January 1, 2000. http://www.nwf.org/News-and-Magazines/National-Wildlife/Animals/Archives/2000/Big-on-Figs.aspx

Kline, Katie. "The Story of the Fig and Its Wasp." Ecological Society of America, May 20, 2011. http://www.esa.org/esablog/research/the-story-of-the-fig-and-its-wasp/

Lewis, Madeleine. "Cuppa & Chat With . . . Dr. Russ Mittermeier, World's Biggest Lemur Fan!" Virgin Unite, Oct. 31, 2014. http://www.virgin.com/unite/leadership-and-advocacy/cuppa-chat-with-dr-russ-mittermeier-worlds-biggest-lemur-fan

Luzynski, Kenneth Cody, Emily Margaret Sluzas, and Megan Marie Wallen. "Pteropodidae: Old World Fruit Bats." University of Michigan Museum of Zoology, *Animal Diversity Web*, April 19, 2009. http://animaldiversity.org/accounts/Pteropodidae/

Markus, Nicola. "'Foxes' That Fly." *International Wildlife*, July/August 2001, vol. 31, issue 4, p. 22. Ebsco Host, Academic Search Elite.

Maryland Department of Natural Resources, Wildlife and Heritage Service. "White-Tailed Deer Biology (*Odocoileus virginianus*)." http://dnr2.maryland.gov/wildlife/Pages/hunt_trap/wtdeerbiology.aspx

Mertl-Millhollen, A.S., K. Blumenfeld-Jones, S.M. Raharison, D.R. Tsaramanana, H. Rasamimanana. "Tamarind Tree Seed Dispersal by Ring-Tailed Lemurs." *Primates*, October 2011, pp. 391-396. http://www.ncbi.nlm.nih.gov/pubmed/21629992

Michels, T.R. "White-Tailed Deer Communication." Trinity Mountain Outdoors. http://www.trmichels.com/WhitetailCommunication.htm

Moisset, Beatriz. "Fig Wasps." United States Department of Agriculture, Forest Service. http://www.fs.fed.us/wildflowers/

pollinators/pollinator-of-the-month/fig_
wasp.shtml

National Park Service. "Redwood National and
State Parks: Directions." http://www.nps.
gov/redw/planyourvisit/directions.htm

New Hampshire Fish and Game. "White-Tailed
Deer (*Odocoileus virginianus*)." http://www.
wildlife.state.nh.us/wildlife/profiles/deer.html

Ogunkunle, A.T.J., and F.A. Oladele. "Leaf
Epidermal Studies in Some Nigerian Species
of *Ficus* L. (Moraceae)." *Plant Systematics
and Evolution*, vol. 274,
pp. 209-221, June 24, 2008. https://www.
unilorin.edu.ng/publications/oladele/
LEAF%20EPIDERMAL%20STUDIES%20
IN%20SOME%20NIGERIAN%20
SPECIES%20OF%20FICUS%20L.%20.pdf

Olson, David F. Jr., Douglass F. Roy, and Gerald
A. Walters. "*Sequoia sempervirens* (D.
Don) Endl.: Redwood." In Russell M. Burns
and Barbara H. Honkala. *Silvics of North
America*, Volume 1. Washington, DC: US
Department of Agriculture, Forest Service,
1990. http://www.na.fs.fed.us/pubs/silvics_
manual/Volume_1/sequoia/sempervirens.
htm

Pennyslvania Game Commission. "A Keystone
Species of the Keystone State." http://www.
depweb.state.pa.us/portal/server.
pt/document/707284/4_a_keystone_
species_pdf

Rooney, T.P. "Deer Impacts on Forest
Ecosystems: A North American Perspective."
Forestry, vol. 74, no. 3, 2001, pp. 201-208.
http://www.botany.wisc.edu/waller/PDFs/
Rooney2001.pdf

Royal Botanic Gardens & Domain Trust.
"Flying-Foxes." http://www.rbgsyd.nsw.
gov.au/welcome/royal_botanic_garden/
gardens_and_domain/wildlife/flying-foxes

San Diego Zoo Global. "Ring-Tailed Lemur
(*Lemur catta*) Fact Sheet, 2009." Updated
February 25, 2015. http://ielc.libguides.
com/sdzg/factsheets/ringtailedlemur

San Francisco Botanical Garden. "What
Are Cloud Forests?" http://www.
sfbotanicalgarden.org/cf/cf/

Save the Redwoods League. "Coast Redwoods."
http://www.savetheredwoods.org/redwoods/
coast-redwoods/

Save the Redwoods League. "Past, Present and
Future of Redwoods: A Redwood Ecology &
Climate Symposium." 2013. https://www.
savetheredwoods.org/wp-content/uploads/
RCCI-Symposium-2013-Abstracts.pdf

Save the Redwoods League. "What Limits
Redwood Height?" http://www.
savetheredwoods.org/grant/what-limits-
redwood-height/

Shanahan, Mike, Samson So, Stephen G.
Compton, and Richard Corlett. "Fig-Eating
by Vertebrate Frugivores: A Global Review."
Biological Reviews, 2001, vol. 76,
pp. 529-572.

Shea, Neil. "Living on a Razor's Edge." *National
Geographic*, November 2009. http://ngm.
nationalgeographic.com/2009/11/stone-
forest/shea-text

State Government Victoria, Department of
Environment and Primary Industries.
"Flying-Foxes." http://www.depi.vic.gov.
au/environment-and-wildlife/wildlife
/flying-foxes

Stier, Sam C., and Tammy L. Mildenstein.
"Dietary Habits of the World's Largest Bats:
The Philippine Flying Foxes, *Acerodon
jubatus* and *Pteropus vampyrus lanensis*."
Journal of Mammalogy, 2005, vol. 86, no.
4, pp. 719-728.

Tree Climbers International. "Guidelines for
Safe Climbing." http://treeclimbing.com/
index.php/climbing/rules

FURTHER READING

Britton, Tamara L. *Flying Fox Bats*. Edina,
MN: ABDO Publishing Company, 2011.

Duke, Kate. *In the Rainforest*. New York:
HarperCollins, 2014.

French, Susannah Terrell. *Operation Redwood*.
New York: Amulet Books, 2009.

Marsico, Katie. *White-Tailed Deer*. New York:
Scholastic Library Publishing, 2014.

Oluonye, Mary N. *Madagascar*. Minneapolis:
Lerner Publishing Group, 2010.

Riley, Joelle. *Ring-Tailed Lemurs*.
Minneapolis: Lerner Publishing Group,
2009.

ON THE INTERNET

Animal Planet: White-Tail Deer (video)
http://www.animalplanet.com/tv-shows/
other/videos/amazing-animal-videos-
white-tail-deer/

BBC Two: Fig Facts (video)
http://www.bbc.co.uk/programmes/
p00485t4

National Geographic: Flying Foxes (video)
http://video.nationalgeographic.com/video/
weirdest-flying-fox

National Geographic: World's Tallest Tree
(video)
http://natgeotv.com/uk/worlds-tallest-tree/
videos/redwoods

National Wildlife Federation: Ring-Tailed
Lemurs
http://www.nwf.org/Kids/Ranger-Rick/
Animals/Mammals/Ringtail-Lemurs.aspx

Save the Redwoods League: Redwoods
Learning Center
http://education.savetheredwoods.org/
kit/kids.php

GLOSSARY

adapt (uh-DAPT)—to adjust to a change in conditions or environment

canopy (KAN-uh-pee)—the cover formed by the leafy upper branches of the trees in a forest

carnivorous (kahr-NIV-er-uhs)—meat-eating

condense (kuhn-DENS)—change from a vapor to a liquid

conservation (kon-ser-VEY-shuhn)—saving from injury or loss

decompose (dee-kuhm-POHZ)—to rot or to break down

disperse (dih-SPURS)—to scatter something in various directions

echolocation (ek-oh-loh-KEY-shun)—the method of sensing and locating objects that an animal uses by making sounds that bounce off of the object and then return to the animal's ears

ecosystem (EE-koh-sis-tuhm)—a system of interaction of the plants and animals in a community

forb (fawrb)—a broad-leaved plant that is not a grass or sedge, such as a clover or sunflower

fungus (FUHNG-guhs; plural **fungi**: FUHNG-gahy)—a life form that lives by breaking down living material such as wood; yeast, molds, and mushrooms are fungi

genus (JEE-nuhs)—a group of species with common characteristics

habitat (HAB-i-tat)—the natural environment that a plant or animal lives in

heartwood (HAHRT-wood)—the hard wood at the center of a tree trunk

home range—the area that a specific animal or group of animals considers its home area and usually stays within

native (NEY-tiv)—currently living in the place where it originally lived (as in a species of plant or animal)

nutrient (NOO-tree-uhnt)—substance that promotes life and good health in the body, particularly in food

porous (PAWR-uhs)—full of tiny holes which allow water or air to pass through

rodent (ROHD-nt)—a group of mammals that gnaw or nibble, including mice, squirrels, and beavers

roost—to sit or rest on a perch, usually for sleep

snout—the part of an animal that contains its nose and jaws

stately (STEYT-lee)—majestic or elegant in appearance and manner

INDEX

About the Author

Bonnie Hinman has loved studying nature since she was a child growing up on her family's farm. Today she is a certified Missouri Master Naturalist and works in her community educating children and adults about the natural world around them. She also volunteers her time to restore and maintain the local ecosystem. Hinman has had more than thirty books published including Mitchell Lane's *Threat to the Leatherback Turtle*. She lives with her husband Bill in Joplin, Missouri, near her children and five grandchildren.